The Little Old House by Anna Wickham

To ALICE and GEOFFREY HARPER

Anna Wickham was the main pseudonym used by Edith Alice Mary Harper who was born on 7th May 1883, Wimbledon, Surrey.

Her first poetry collection was published privately in 1911 under another pseudonym, John Oland. Appropriately enough it was called Songs by John Oland. The main theme of the book was the difficulties of relationships between men and women. Unfortunately, her possessive husband was very upset at her publication, having also shown little support for her earlier singing and acting careers. It led to violent quarrels and sadly Anna had a nervous breakdown and was admitted to a private psychiatric hospital for a period of six weeks.

Shortly after recovering, she met Harold Monro at his Poetry Bookshop. He encouraged her writing, and this led to a second collection being published in 1915. Her life now became increasingly split between domesticity and the yearned for bohemian life that was now calling her.

Whilst the poetry volumes she released are small in number she left behind several hundred unpublished poems that survived both the war and her life. Today she is regarded as a leading Modernist poet who was able to frankly express her desires and feelings through verse despite these often being at odds with the prevailing morals of the day.

Index of Contents

THE LITTLE OLD HOUSE

Now the house of your Grandfather Hardy
Was a scented Shropshire farm,
Where a boy might dream in the cinders,
Without a thought of harm,
For he who is burnt finds ointment
As soon as he understands
And the sting of a burn may be welcomed
For the healing of certain hands.

O the hands of your Grandmother Hardy
Were lovely and strong and white.
For she rubbed on their red with goose grease

After her prayers at night.
And they were free in giving
Yet never gave too much;
And not a baby living
Could cry beneath their touch.

Now the faith of your Grandfather Hardy
Was burning and clear and keen;
His heart was like his homestead
Ordered and straight and clean;
And when his work was ended,
Because the light grew dim,
Stole out of the clear cut shadows
A lovely English hymn.

O the love of your Grandmother Hardy
Was good as farm-house bread;
For all that was strong she worshipped,
And all that was weak she led.
And when her man was wounded
By a stray shot on his land,
She chid her eyes for weeping
But could not raise her hand.

Then take the tinker's road my son
Or sit in the courts of kings,
Yet carry from your mother
These two most royal things;
Let the faith of your Grandfather Hardy
Stand for your pride in life;
Let the hands of your Grandmother Hardy
Conduct you to your wife.

THE FREEING

True Love came to the Sleepers' town,
Wandering up and wandering down,
I'm looking for the man I know is there
Hidden with cowardice, hidden with care,
Behind false looks and behind false speech,
I will have him out and throne him within reach
Of all men's honour for all men's aid,
And Time shall acclaim the king that I have made.
Such a king we have met, you and I, in a dream,
For we two know, you are not the slave you seem
But a most royal prisoner to whom I bring release
That you may have God's laughter, and I may have
God's peace.

PORTRAIT OF A BOY

Here is a silvery beauty, like the sheen
Of dandy clocks and daisies on new green,
And yet his skin has meshed the sun's full light,
And he has gold to aureole his white.

As pure as peace the moulding of his face,
His eyes' clear blue is tint of courtesy,
And on his cheeks' dinted most rosy place,
Sleep, near the full rose mouth,
Young loves to be.

His slim arched feet are swift as nesting birds,
His body lissom as a willow wand,
And little brooks leap laughing through his words,
And like a sporting squirrel, his brown hand.

A BOY'S VOICE

So lovely is his voice to me,
That I imagine a young tree
To rain a golden dew
More sweet to taste than wine.
Each perfect yellow sphere
Is as a word I hear
A sunny note, from the young throat
Of this white boy of mine.

REPRIEVE

I am heavy with my secret
And with uneasy happiness.
Here's too much joy for sense to bear!
From rapture is my weariness.

That he should love so true and well
After estranged long years!
if my pride would let me tell
My glad relief in tears.

So old is my dumb misery
I cannot hope to weep;
Then come Oblivion cover me
Let me go hence, and sleep.

SENTIMENTS

Windswept from where they grew
These tender flowers lie dead:
How many things were true
Had they been left unsaid.

EMBASSY

All the great lovely house
When he's away,
Is like a bush
From which the rose is torn.
Is like a songless thrush
A flowerless May
Is like a gemless crown
A sunless morn.
Have you not marked him and his pageantry
Grace and the pleasure which I lack?
Hut he has left a gallant guard with me:
I will send Love, to drive him back.

THE OPEN DOOR

Opening my door to sun and scented wind
I saw Spring moving in the apple boughs—
The vision of your beauty came into my mind
Your hands, your throat, your mouth, and your fine moulded brows.

It were as wise to shut you from my soul
As from my house to ban the air and light.
Then come you in! and live my blest control:
I draw the bolt. It is no longer night.

THE TWO KINGS

To an eloquent friend I had given the key
Of my heart and my house and my granary;
He flung my heart for his dogs to eat,
And the shift of my soul he spread for his feet,
And freely he squandered my loveliest thing,
He would have me allow him the pride of a king.

Because of his kingliness was I so poor,
That I knocked for an alms at my silent friend's door.

Sham'dly and sadly I told him my needs,
And he said "Long ago friend I gave you two seeds
Which I hid in my garden and now they are grown,
One tree is my wage, and the other your own."
Then courteous he led me, "Come hither and see."
The gardener had nurtured a magical tree,
For the fruit was of gold and the trunk was of jade
So I mended the wreck which my false friend had made.

NAMING THE GIRL

Soon after I was five, my dear
We lived beside the sea,
And I had such an angry nurse
She took the shells from me
She hid the crinkly shells away,
For the small faults of yesterday.

And even smiling was a sin!
Nurse took a brush and scrubbed my skin-
And when her nasty work was done
They found my brownness was the sun
And then she coughed and scolded me
For all I did in Italy.

And we'd a great tall house
With shadows on the stairs
And devils in the corners
Who popped out after prayers.
I can see them now my dear
Though I am nearly old,
But once in that house garden
I found a marigold.

And O it looked so happy!
And O it shone so sweet!
I ran up through the shadows
With dancing in my feet,
And I polka-ed in the schoolroom
When nurse was at her tea;
I didn't hear her scolding
When she remembered me.

And when your Mother told me
Her beautiful surprise,
I thought about my marigold

From pleasure in her eyes,
I said " If it's a little girl
Who comes to live with you,
Be kind and call her Marigold
After the one I knew."

CAROL

When little Jesus slept
Unguarded in a stable
Out of the grass a Daisy crept
As close as he was able,
And watched the babe with steady eye
While following bees droned lullaby
"Day's eye, Day's eye, thou blest day's eye."
Happy was Mary in that hour
At service from so low a flower.

And Cherubim at night
Flew with the tale to God
Who touched the flower from Heaven's height
With a great shining rod
And in the morning it is told
That daisy woke a marigold.
"Mary's gold, O Mary's gold,"
Yet more than gold that mother mild
Loved a flower's kindness to her child.

BIOLOGY FOR BREAKFAST

(Nine hundred and ninety ninth type of domestic argument)

Why does the peacock spread his jewelled tail,
And walk so proud a prince of gentlemen?
Has he not hopes his beauty will prevail
With that small critical brown hen?

Why does the throstle clear his mellow throat,
Till all the wood a magic draught receives?
Has he not faith some individual note
May yet convince Herself among the leaves?

Think of the tiger and his fiery zest,
Of all hot fights the wilds among,
If she who waits approves not of the test
She'll brook the lover, but devour his young.

Good scientist, review all things alive,
And for male strength and beauty you will find
If not a cause a fixed co-relative
Within the female mind.

In all creative will has done
This female judgment was God's tool
And yet my Lord you'll take my son
And send him to a public school!

Burn me the cities! Raze this little height,
Clear its complexity, and then
Give me my pride, my ancient natural right
To breed you men!

THE LUTE

I am Love's lute; I am thine instrument
When thou art mute, then am I discontent,
The wedded song of us shall rule the flood
And tame the whirlwind in its wildest mood.

For at thy singing must my heart afford
Its natural music, a sustaining chord:
Then strike, O Troubadour, these pliant strings
And walk most mighty through the arch of kings.

THE LITTLEST GIRL

Here's a small woman
So absurdly young,
She is not well-acquainted
With her tongue!
Finger goes in
Exploring all about
Then with the rosy tongue
Comes wandering out,
Travels awhile
Along the rosier lips:
Time for a smile!
So back the hermit slips
And head aside
Like a full rose on stalk
Her eyes are wide
To hear the giant's talk.

THE PERFORMANCE

When we played a Greek play to the poor,
A fat old woman quickly sought the door.
She looked like a sad black beetle in her old shawl,
A creature that one could not educate at all.
I shall go back to Plaistow before long,
And sing that woman just a silly funny song.

PLEASURE OF WORDS

As a tired man
Throws himself down on sun-warmed grass;
As the lips of a babe
Close fervently at the kind breast;
As a man starved for love
Knows the dear contact of his woman's body,
So and with fuller rapture the poet remembers
Life and the pleasure that is in speech.

WORK OF JAMES AND THE NATION BUILDERS

Jim's a lad that's stout and bold,
Five days more than five years old;
What craft shall this craftsman choose?
He'll wash the hearth and brush the shoes.

Brushing shoes is the queer boy's fun
Yet Master James is a gentleman's son;
There's a trade for the squire to choose
Washing hearths and brushing shoes!

P'raps it's the fault of the poor lad's nurse
That he won't remember that work's a curse,
Maybe his Mother's one whit to blame
That he will believe that work's a game.

All his young life he has never been sick
His eyes are clear and his fingers quick
He's free as a king, and hale as a peasant
His body tells him that work is pleasant.

Who knows but our world has read amiss
The splendid myth of Genesis!
For God can never curse the ground
When man's heart is high and his body sound.

Then let our nobler age confess
God's curse on slattern weariness!
Cursed be such sloth, and let it be desired
That no child ail, so man be never tired.

More blest than Eden is our world of sin
Since curious cleansings can be wrought therein
Then let our pride contrive a thousand games,
To search and scour with all the zest of James.

STUDY OF A CERTAIN BRILLIANT YOUNG ACTRESS

She can never do her Duty,
She remembers the people who taught her music
When she was a child;
Then from a ravished sense of beauty
She becomes so self-conscious
That she runs wild.
She can't work
She functions like a flower or a wheel.
Even in art
She never knows, she can only feel.
Leave her alone
She will accomplish what God meant
She'll give you something perfect
As a roses's scent.

HOST

When I was host to my enemy
I set him a chair of state
I summoned a solemn company
And served him quails on gold plate,
I pledged him courteous all the night
And this I did for spite.

There was little enough of my pride to see
When I was host to my friend,
I set him a dish of hominy
The feast came quick to an end.
I said "It is here I have lost my skin
Since I was a hardy fool
Then open your counsel and let me come in
To school myself at your school."

With the blood of my wounds I pledged my friend

And fitly I had proved
Before that grim carousal's end
How courteous I had loved.

THE HOUSE OF LITTLE VICTORIES

The house is barred unto the lover.
His foot shall not pass over
Stone of this threshold-
Though fires be fierce within
The living heart is cold.
This house is open to all covert sin
Free to the poor light mind,
But thou Desirer Come not in!
'Tis thou wilt loose and bind.
This is the house of an eternal sloth
And they who live therein are loth
To sting and wake.
Leave thou this dwelling
For thy kingship's sake.

MEG AND THE WITCH WIGHT

Muddly Meg was ever toiling
With all her poor thin ugly will,
Muddly Meg was ever spoiling
Muddly Meg was never still.

Meg was working at her children
She took no gracious thought to please,
Meg was working at her baby,
She never stopt to kiss his knees;
Meg was working at her husband
Till that poor man ran mad one day:
He said " I'll go and fetch a witch-wight
There's one sells pipes across the way.

Thither he came the merry master
Covered the vizen with a motley dress
He said "Thou fountain of disaster
Thou mother of foul idleness,
Stifler of men, ill architect of children,
Follow pale misery. Come shake a leg!
And they went dancing down our village
The mystery man, and merry Meg.

STATESWOMAN AND THE HOUSE

Were there dynamic in a pure democracy
The servants in this house would not reflect my mood;
When I'm all inky with my poetry
No thing is found where it but lately stood.

When I'm not willing all this house runs ill
Since for fulfilling I advance the will,
I am their slave, since they will never rule for me:
That I'll not have, and they shall go to school for me.

Thus I'll compel them, thus they shall be free.
All power applied conditions liberty
And the full power of life shall not be known,
Till through their freedom, I attain my own.

SONG FOR DOMESTIC ANGUISH

Give me a house where the servants sing,
Fit it with green baize doors
So that the faults of their carolling
Stop at the servants' floors.
Ingenious Love shall bring to pass
This happy Reconstruction,
Stating the difference betwixt class and class
Not in Joy, but in Voice-production.

DUE FOR HOSPITALITY

(To H.M.)

God is a courteous gentleman
And a most genial host.
Such could not rest
If any guest
Should leave his house to roast!
Then fear not Hell!
Respect God well:
He's great as man at least.
Before you're dead,
See there is spread,
Within your life a feast,
Which it is meet
That you should eat,
With courtesy expressed.

Acclaim with mirth
God's pleasant earth,
As fits a gracious guest.

THE FAIRY WIFE

When you have gathered a thousand pound
I'll not let you kiss me,
I'll steal out of the garden bound
And you will never miss me
You'll buy a farm with your minted gold,
And drowse o'er the fire, as you grow old.

Slippery slippery spending Jack
What wealth would you gather? What gold could you keep?
You'd had scarcely a coat for your great broad back,
If I had not charmed you full half asleep
When the good grain's in the great oak box
I'm through the edges as lithe as a fox.

Love! Love! Love, I'm tired of the name
Mine is the wound and yours is the balm
I'm to a duck pond to drown the flame,
When you are master of yon hill-farm.
Sleep sounder sounder slippery Jack,
And quickly gather the gold you lack.

It is my pleasure to walk alone
On the sheer steep above the snow,
I have a cave and a bed of my own
On the blue height where lichens grow,
There I will sing with the deeps to hear
While the stars keep their courses nor swing too near.

THE HOMECOMING

I waited ten years in the husk
That once had been our home
Waiting from dawn till dusk
To see if he would come.

And there he was beside me
Always at board and bed,
I looked and woe betide me
He whom I loved was dead.

He fell at night on the hill side,

They brought him home to his place;
I had not the solace of sorrow
Until I had looked in his face.

Then I clutched the broken body,
To see if he stirred or moved,
For there in the smile of his dying
Was the gallant man I had loved.

O wives come lend me your weeping
I have not enough of tears,
For he is dead who was sleeping
These ten accursed years.

THE SONG OF THE OLD MOTHER

Do you remember the summer
Before the boy was born?
You rowed me up the river,
Between the filling' corn,
I see you now as you smiled at me
And handed me ashore
Then we were happier lovers,
Than in the year before.

We wandered in the orchard
Beside the river brink
I saw the young bronze apples
And lingered there to think.
"The child will be here in the autumn,
When fruit is red on the boughs."
You asked me why I was smiling
As we went into the house.

The last thing I saw from my windows
Were ladders against the trees
Then I woke on my happiest morning
To see your son on your knees,
And I was weak for laughing
But there were tears in my joy
To see yourself a father
And you a slip of a boy.

And he was brave and wholesome
Like apples. As he began
He always was and shall be
Your son is a splendid man.
But sure I was never his mother,
For you are my only child,

The lad who stood in the orchard
To help me ashore, and smiled.

REACTION

A certain bitter shrew
Gained sudden courtesy
Until a wonder grew,
That such a change should be.

Said that poor man her mate,
"This thing can not endure."
And the priest came out in state
Scenting miraculous cure.

He asked "How is't my child
You who were harsh of old
Are now so douce and mild
And are no more a scold?"

Then did her quick tears start
"I am grown sudden kind,
Since I saw a man of great heart,
And of most gallant mind."

COUNSEL TO CRAFTSWOMEN

Deep in the man there is a lonely boy
To life's hard nurture still unreconciled
Starving for beauty and for natural joy:
Go thou kind woman, and console the child!

There is new truth concealed in this day's night
And man shall find it with a boy's keen eyes
Thine honour is in victory for his sight:
Feed then the child in him if thou art wise.

Make of thy love a pleasant laughing game
And set thy beauty like a birth day feast
Be thou first mother, who art wife in name:
So is his man-hood grown, his power increased.

Yet, for that manhood call him not "My son "
But at his weakest honour him in word.
So shall a play-boy when the game is done
Prove thy most true and honourable lord!

Where hast thou hid thee
My most dear delight?
When my heart bid thee
Thou cam'st not in sight.
I thought Love held a happy wizardry
So to rule chance
That he'd deliver thee.

Fortune's a cheat
Since she withholds my dear
We may not meet
Through all this heavy year;
Silent I wait
For I will never call thee
I'll yet rule Chance
That sudden joy befall me.

Beauty's no mime
To heed a prompter's call
She'll choose her time
Or she'll not come at all.
I'll to my grave
Without our happy meeting
Rather than wound thee
With unlovely greeting.

Lacking his presence
What is left for me?
I'll find his essence
His dear quality.
By sheltered tarns
Where the spent sea-wind dies
There is the stillness
Of my lover's eyes.

Where a full sea
Beats steady to the sand
There is the strength
And beauty of his hand.
In the deep wood's
Most fragrant holy place,
There is his scent
His mystery and his grace.

In the hot heart of song
In the bright soul of story
There is the shadow

Of my lover's glory.
In all there is
For pleasure and for pride,
There does the spirit
Of my love abide.

Come thou discover me
Lest I should be betrayed
To lose thy substance
Beauty's but thy shade.
Dear, rule thou Chance
For such is my good faith
I love thee living
More than any wraith!

SONG OF THE EXALTED

This child's father is a strong man, is a valiant man
He is God's man.
He is lord of anvils, hammers and fierce fires
With his great hand he fashions a brass pan
And he shall spill in it world's hungers, world's desires.

This child's father is a strong man, is a valiant man
He is God's man.
He shall stretch his sinewy back and shall exalt the pan
Brimming with tears and grimy sweat and grief
He shall fling it to the stars, for the old world's relief
Till the black liquor sinks through crevices of night
And the assaulted dome crashes an answering light.

This child's father is a strong man, is a valiant man
He is God's man.
I am more blest than any other
Since he has called me
For his proud heir's mother.

THE PLEADER

Love has compelled me subtly to offend
He, who is very Prince of Courtesy
And for his fault I cannot make amend,
I am your suppliant for charity.

How meek is Love, who thus will be a mime
To learn if faith be worthy of delight;
How proud! He will not leave the test to Time

He swoops to knowledge like a spear in flight.

Love has compelled me to forego my will
My tongue turns traitor to my heart and mind
If you believe of me my feigned ill
I must forswear you, since you are not kind.

House of all dear Desires There is no cost
But I would pay it to abide in you.
Then yield your little debt, lest all be lost:
Pay in blind loyalty Love's chosen due.

THE BOY AND THE PLAYHOUSE

Give him two sticks a flower and a stone,
And the small model of a sheep,
And such a fairy land will be his own,
As you'll not find in waking or in sleep.

Blind educationist, take your proper way!
And never teach a little child to play!
God send our theatre new phantasies,
As fresh and exquisite as his.

FELICITY NEAT

Felicity Neat the serving maid
Cleared the muddle Queen Order made,
Smoothed her silver dress away
In scented leaves of yesterday,
Then turned a musical handle round
Till people danced to the pleasant sound.
Queen Order laughed to their chiming feet:
O how I love you, Felicity Neat.

TIDINESS AND ORDER

Where work is always finished
And nothing ever strays,
There are the sad old children
And the wet empty days.

There are too many servants
So every day is long
And duty fills all silence

And leaves no room for song.

In the house of beautiful Order
Everything has its place,
But a boy may run out of the schoolroom
To kiss his Mother's face.

THE BOY AND THE SCRAPHEAP

Let us find the truth of Stephen
Since God has set the seed of him
So honouring our service
Till man shall have his need of him.
Can we understand his essence
Know the secret of his joy?
Here a woman and her husband
Are joined within a boy.

See his straight lovely body
As he runs across the field!
There is his Mother's courage,
Clear written and revealed,
And his face has flowers and marbles
And stars and firefly light
For he stole his father's spirit
In the silence of the night.

A fairy boy is Stephen
And warden of such gold
That what he steals is given
Again a thousand fold;
I flung him sticks and rubble
For the pleading of his eyes,
And there among the stubble
He built a paradise.

What need have such as Stephen
For a beauty clear defined?
For the Mother of all perfectness
Sits throned within his mind.
There is Old Wit the huntress
With her brave dogs in hand
And Stephen shall unleash them
To riot through his land.

And where he runs they follow
Hosanna, for the chase!
For see, within what hollow
They make their sporting place!

Not among flocks and beehives
Not on the beach or down,
But on a builder's scrapheap,
Of this erroneous town.

THE VAIN GIRL

When you left me last night
I dressed myself in shiny white;
I wore my simplest satin dress
Knowing you love my slenderness.
And I was like an ivory snake
And I was this for Beauty's sake.

NOTE

A fine spirit of hospitality
Has disregard for property
And fine contempt of quality.
It offers all things easy-found and rare
Without words, without apparent care,
As God almighty offers "sun and air.

QUEEN'S SONG ON SAINT VALENTINE'S DAY

Here are we You and I
Waiting, waiting!
While the happy birds flash by
Swift to their mating.
In March will fledgelings be in nest
In March I'll lay my babe to rest
On the knees of the king.
O happy Mother! and O happy Spring!

What shall we do, you and I
Waiting, waiting?
We will bless the birds that fly
Swift to their mating
And through the house we'll gather wool and thread,
That Mistress Thrush mav build a royal bed
For her brave children, who will dream of flight
When you my babe, have joy of light.

Thanks for your song good thrush
You cheer our waiting.

See I have laid you wool beneath this bush
God bless your mating.

SONG

There is one lovely! There is one kind
Of gracious heart, and of delicious mind!
And to my mortal flesh immortal joys are given
Since he is not withheld from me by any coward's Heaven

But he shall walk and talk with me
Through these unhonoured ways
To sanctify this town to me
And hallow all my days.

THE ETERNAL FAITH

Thou art established in my endless love
Firm as a hill is set upon a plain,
The little torrents leap, the great winds move:
Thou shalt fear changes as the heights fear rain.

My faith shall hold thee in thy chosen way
Sure as that will which binds the stars in place.
Would'st thou mistrust me? Wait that final day
When hills lack bases, and when suns doubt space.

TO JANE-ACROSS-THE-BAY

When my blossomy tree came out in May
To the edge of the sea I took my way
And set a flowery twig afloat:
I thought white petals the sails of a boat
And dreamed kind winds would bring it to land
Where rosy feet touch happy sand.
A flower went down in the foam of the sea,
But a gallant ship was lost to me.

YOUNG MISTRESS MARIGOLD

She is so courteous, she is so wise
She wakes every morning with joy in her eyes,
To bless with her smiles what we say, what we do,

And honour our loving the whole day through.

Her cheeks are rose red, and her body snow white
I found a new pearl in her lips last night
Will my heart burst for love of such gems flowers and snows!
For she is all-sweet, and she grows and she grows.

SOOTHSAYER

Take heed! Thou lovest in the king's pale daughter
The shadow of thyself in a still pool.
When thou hast riddled this, curse not the water,
Nor scorn thyself for a bedazzled fool.
Therein 's thy Godhead. Thou art more than human
To raise such dreads, from such a silly woman.

SONG

I will sing no more of Love
Love shall sing in me,
I will sing the bird in the grove,
The flower the fish and the bee,
For I love well small things that dwell
On land and in the sea.

INVOCATION TO THE INTELLIGENCE OF A GENTLEMAN

Nymph in a Cloud!
Shy loiterer on a height!
By faith art thou avowed
Thou art not known to sight;
Pity the clod in me,
Frail denizen of air;
I, lacking sight of thee,
Must doubt if thou art there!

LIGHT, THE DAUGHTER OF CHARITY

Light, the daughter of Charity
Kissed her servants and made them free,
Staunched the wounds of their mad carouse
With holy oil of her Father's house
Then harried them back to Charity,

To sweep in her cupboards and find a key.

Thus she came to her power at length,
Loosed from their bonds young Beauty and Strength;
"Hear, my sons! for your Mother is wise,
Sorrow has fed her ears and her eyes,
But you for your joy shall be wiser than she,"
Said Light the daughter of Charity.

"Beauty, thy scent shall be truer than Truth,
In strength shall abide eternal youth,
And he shall steal from that poisoner Night
A lovelier gem than the jewel of Light:"
Thus said the daughter of Charity
Who swept in her cupboards and found a key.

ON THE DAY THEY TOOK DOWN THE GRILLE

(House of Commons, 1917)

Now give me a high room and a long taper
Much ink and pens and endless reams of paper,
Then I might well my lyric mettle prove,
For I have made a peace with my true-love.
How were my singing more than raucous din,
With fires and tempests raging fierce within?
I cannot raise a paradise from me
Without some seedlings from reality.
If ever I speak truth or I sing clear
Impute it to my love, that he is dear,
If I show gallantry in any fight
Know a man's courage was his wife's delight,
If I walk comely know a woman's grace
Is but the image of her lover's face.
Go black-cat Misery avoid my pages
Hence clammy Passion with your bombast rages
Tell me some hen bird sings upon her tree
And I will raise a natural melody
But if male singing is by God preferred
I will learn silence from the nobler bird.

DEDICATION OF THE COOK

If any ask why there's no great She-Poet,
Let him come live with me, and he will know it:
If I'd indite an ode or mend a sonnet,
I must go choose a dish or tie a bonnet;

For she who serves in forced virginity
Since I am wedded will not have me free;
And those new flowers my garden is so rich in
Must die for clammy odours of my kitchen.

Yet had I chosen Dian's barrenness
I'm not full woman, and I can't be less,
So could I state no certain truth for life,
Can I survive and be my good man's wife?

Yes! I will make the servant's cause my own
That she in pity leave me hours alone
So I will tend her mind and feed her wit
That she in time have her own joy of it;
And count it pride that not a sonnet's spoiled
Lacking her choice betwixt the baked and boiled.
So those young flower my garden is so rich in
Will blossom from the ashes of my kitchen!

THE WOMAN AND THE AEROPLANE

Here I stand in this muddy Street
While a great plane goes by!
There is a rage of dancing in my feet
And in my heart a mad-ecstatic cry
"He is up! He is out!
Brave on supremest enterprise
With a swift menace all about
He cleaves new skies
Insistent as that engine is his mood;
I know it by the leaping of my blood!"

LITTLE MOUSE MIASMA

I'll tell you what the Fairy did
Who feared the shocking mouse,
She fed her fire with wurzel-skins
And spoiled her lovely house
And smoked out all her house my dear
For a wizard small as that
Although his secret would be clear
To any common cat.

Now I'm a horrid giant dear
As every child can see,
And soon the horrid smoke will clear,
And all because of me!

For I will kill the shocking mouse
With this small stick I hold
And then the fairy's lovely house
Will shine like gems and gold.

THE THRIFTY LOVER

She is so exquisite! I will go hence
To make a singing of her eminence
For if her living lips should touch my skin
Such sweet commotion would abide therein
That I were no more diligent and no more wise

Than to breathe out my happy life in sighs.
For very fear of her I'll go my way
Yet bare her beauty in my heart each day;
A richer treasure shall I win from this
Than will a hardier man who waits to kiss:
From such chaste intercourse might well be got
Songs that will live when she and I are not.

EYES AND THE CHILD

Looking from out the gates of paradise
The Holy Child perceived the devil;
Long he regarded him with pitying eyes,
Then said "Thou art no ugly thing of evil
But a great angel sorely tired
Then come thou, eat and sleep within."
The devil followed as the babe desired:
That was the end of sin.

THE MIRROR

'Twas on the eve of Christmas day
I had not hope nor charity
I met a beggar on my way
Who stretched his hand and grinned at me
I went into my house and barred the door
"He is not poor as I am poor."

'Twas on the morn of Christmas day
Bankrupt in heart and sick in mind
O'er heath and wild I took my way
In haste to leave Myself behind

When on the hill I paused for breath
I found that beggar still as death.

He said "Oh thou that art a cold
With fiercer rigours than this blast
I sue for neither warmth nor gold
But this redeeming gift at last
A soul of your good charity
And grant a spirit room in thee."

'Twas at the noon of Christmas day
The sun was at his little height
And I went singing on my way
Singing for freedom and delight
The mendicant who walked with me
Sustained a happy harmony.

And on the night of Christmas day
We two walked homeward through the gloom
Into the house I led the way
To show him to my inner room
'Twas then a wonder came to pass
He waited in the looking-glass.

Then I had almost shrieked for fear
That madness should abide with me
I turned about and I am here
My living comrade laughed to me
I am Thyself. Myself to Time's end
I am thy friend.

MANUMISSION

Seeing you first, I had such pleasure of you,
As a land-weary sailor has of the smell of the sea,
You were all I had desired through dusty years,
I will not have you bound to such as me.

I am not compelled by your most loving looks,
Nor by those pleasant arts at your command,
But when you disregard me, for your soul's unity
Silent I lay my life within your hands.

Can it be true I love you
Since I would never have you tied to my gown?
I am less happy with you indolent in my sight
Than when I know you busy in the town.

Go you! Free of your love of me

Free of the thriftless fret of small delights
Spend your brave days in fruitful liberty,
I have a dream for every loveless night.

THE DOORKEEPER

Tread soft, ye stars and little winds lie still
My lord Berolf has cut himself a quill
Here on the board is a new parchment spread
And the long taper mocks the silken bed
I will have no owls to hoot among these bushes
No sleeping starlings doves nor thrushes
To change-a-leg-in-the-night and make a creaking
Out bats and mice with scratching and with squeaking
Back to your closes fairies sylphs to your ways
Elves to your hills and goblins to your caves
If near these precincts any woman scold
May a black palsy strike her dumb and old
Our lord Berolf has cut himself a quill
And by his might I bid this night lie still.

MIRACLE

I bring you this word
Truly I was redeemed
Not by God- Withdrawn but by living man
A man bred natural in this town.

He gave me great scope
For my faith and my hope
Since he was not of the scatheless,
But a poor sinner.

He gave me my need
A pod of dream-seed,
And he was not of the scatheless
But a poor sinner.

Such miraculous high things I dreamed of him
That I was quick redeemed of him.
I bring you this word
Truly I was redeemed
Not by God- Withdrawn but by living man
A man bred natural in this town.

Anna Wickham was the main pseudonym used by Edith Alice Mary Harper who was born on 7th May 1883 at 5 The Ridgeway, Wimbledon, Surrey.

Her childhood was chaotic. Her parent's marriage was disordered and her unconventional mother suddenly decided to leave for Australia with the infant Anna. It lasted a year before her Mother contracted pneumonia and Anna was placed in an institution. Her father arranged for them to return to England at some point in 1885.

Anna was encouraged to read and write from an early age but allied with this was their return, in 1890, to Australia. Her mother's teaching and character-reading career as a clairvoyant, Madame Reprah ('Harper' spelt backwards), and her father's many jobs led to an unsettled life.

In Queensland, Anna attended the local convent school followed by All Hallows' School, Brisbane (1894–6) and Sydney Girls' High School (1897–9). She seemed to not be motivated at academic life but had talent as a singer. However, her Father continued to add to her education by discussing philosophy and other subjects with her. In return Anna promised to become a poet. Her Mother meanwhile worked on grammar and elocution with her.

A return to England in 1904, initially to pursue a singing career, was partially successful. She won a drama scholarship before moving to Paris to pursue her singing in 1905.

The following year, 1906, she married a London solicitor, Patrick Hepburn and they settled in Hampstead.

The early years of her marriage were taken up with the raising of her two sons and work with the contemporary philanthropic movement, with a focus on maternal care, at St Pancras Hospital.

Her first poetry collection was published privately in 1911 under another pseudonym, John Oland. Appropriately enough it was called Songs by John Oland. The main theme of the book was the difficulties of relationships between men and women. Unfortunately, her possessive husband was very upset at her publication, having also shown little support for her earlier singing and acting careers. It led to violent quarrels and sadly Anna had a nervous breakdown and was admitted to a private psychiatric hospital for a period of six weeks.

Despite this betrayal, she later reconciled with Hepburn. (They would go on to have two more sons, Richard and George, conceived while Hepburn was on leave from war service in the Royal Naval Air Service and RAF.)

Shortly after recovering, she met Harold Monro at his Poetry Bookshop. He encouraged her writing, and this led to a second collection being published in 1915. Her life now became increasingly split between domesticity and the yearned for bohemian life that was now calling her.

During the War, whilst Hepburn was away, she struck up several literary friendships including with D. H. Lawrence and his wife Frieda. She also knew H. D., (accounts suggest they may have had an affair) and many others in the literary circle of the day.

The tragic death of her son Richard, of scarlet fever at age four, was devastating and she moved to Paris to recuperate but continued to write.

Her marriage now began to fall apart and in 1926 she separated from Hepburn although they reunited in 1928. Hepburn died the following year, 1929, in an accident on holiday. Eerily one of her earlier poems foretells the nature of his death; falling down a mountain.

During the 1930s she was well known in literary London and wrote a great deal of poetry but found it difficult to procure publication. But in 1936 John Gawsworth helped Anna to publish Thirty-Six New Poems.

In 1938 she and other feminists began a group they called the League for the Protection of the Imagination of Women.

During the Second World War her house was bombed and she lost several manuscripts and all of her correspondence.

On 30th April 1947 Anna Wickham hanged herself at the door leading into the garden at 68 Parliament Hill and, rather than a letter by way of explanation, she left a poem.

Whilst the poetry volumes she released are small in number she left behind several hundred unpublished poems that survived both the war and her life. Today she is regarded as a leading Modernist poet who was able to frankly express her desires and feelings through verse despite these often being at odds with the prevailing morals of the day.

Anna Wickham – A Concise Bibliography

Songs of John Oland (1911)
The Contemplative Quarry (1915)
The Man With A Hammer (1916)
The Little Old House 1921